⊦<= [A Math]~±÷
Journey Through
PLANET
EARTH DISCARD

Anne Rooney

Crabtree Publishing Company
www.crabtreebooks.com

Crabtree Publishing Company

www.crabtreebooks.com

1-800-387-7650

Published in Canada
616 Welland Ave.
St. Catharines, ON
L2M 5V6

Published in the United States
PMB 59051, 350 Fifth Ave.
59th Floor,
New York, NY

First published in 2014 by Wayland
(A division of Hachette Children's Books)
Copyright © Wayland 2014

Author: Anne Rooney
Commissioning editor: Debbie Foy
Editorial director: Kathy Middleton
Content Review: Reagan Miller
Editors: Jon Richards, Crystal Sikkens
Consultant: Steve Winney
Designer: Ed Simkins
Prepress technician: Katherine Berti
Print and production coordinator: Katherine Berti

Produced by Tall Tree Ltd

Photographs:
5t Shutterstock.com/Pavel Ilyukhin, 7t Shutterstock.com/Burben, 9t Shutterstock.com/Michael C. Gray, 9b all Shutterstock.com/CataVic, 11t and c Shutterstock.com/banderlog, 12cl both Shutterstock.com/JungleOutThere, 15t Shutterstock.com/ Ammit Jack, 18-19 snowflakes Shutterstock.com/Yulia Glam, 24t Shutterstock.com/Rostislav Ageev, 26c Shutterstock.com/Canoneer, cover Shutterstock.com

The website addresses (URLs) included in this book were valid at the time of going to press. However, it is possible that contents or addresses may have changed since the publication of this book. No responsibility for any such changes can be accepted by either the author or the publisher.

Printed in Hong Kong/082014/BK20140613

Library and Archives Canada Cataloguing in Publication

Rooney, Anne, author
    A math journey through planet Earth / Anne Rooney.

(Go figure!)
Includes index.
Issued in print and electronic formats.
ISBN 978-0-7787-0728-8 (bound).--ISBN 978-0-7787-0736-3 (pbk.).--ISBN 978-1-4271-7664-6 (pdf).--ISBN 978-1-4271-7660-8 (html)

    1. Mathematics--Juvenile literature. 2. Nature conservation--Juvenile literature. I. Title.

QA40.5.R66 2014   j510   C2014-903584-5
                                       C2014-903585-3

Library of Congress Cataloging-in-Publication Data

Rooney, Anne, author.
 A math journey through planet Earth / Anne Rooney.
   pages cm. -- (Go figure!)
 Includes index.
 ISBN 978-0-7787-0728-8 (reinforced library binding) -- ISBN 978-0-7787-0736-3 (pbk.) -- ISBN 978-1-4271-7664-6 (electronic pdf) -- ISBN 978-1-4271-7660-8 (electronic html)
 1. Mathematics--Juvenile literature. 2. Earth (Planet)--Juvenile literature. 3. Earth (Planet)--Miscellanea--Juvenile literature. I. Title.

 QA113.R653 2015
 510--dc23
                                       2014020138

As the leader of an ecological expedition, your job is to use your mathematical knowledge to explore different regions of the world that are affected by natural events, climate change, or human activity.

CONTENTS

04 AROUND THE WORLD

06 ERUPTING GEYSERS

08 FOSSIL HUNTING

10 TAKING FOSSILS HOME

12 GEMSTONES IN POMPEII

14 VOLCANIC THREAT

16 MELTING MOUNTAIN ICE

18 FEELING COLDER

20 MONSOON TIME

22 SNOWED IN!

24 DEEP-SEA DIVING

26 GLOBAL TIME

28 ANSWERS

30 MATH GLOSSARY

32 LEARNING MORE AND INDEX

Words in **bold** appear in the glossary on pages 30–31.

Answers to the Go Figure! challenges can be found on page 28.

Please note: The Imperial and metric systems are used interchangeably throughout this book.

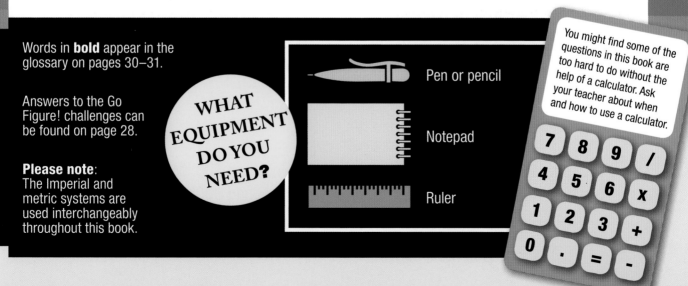

WHAT EQUIPMENT DO YOU NEED?

Pen or pencil

Notepad

Ruler

You might find some of the questions in this book are too hard to do without the help of a calculator. Ask your teacher about when and how to use a calculator.

AROUND THE WORLD

Your first mission takes you to China, where you are looking at how people have moved around over long periods of time.

LEARN ABOUT IT
WORKING WITH LARGE NUMBERS

It is often useful to be able to see which is the larger of two or more numbers. We use the symbols >, <, or = to show how numbers compare.

< means the first number is smaller than the second.   **5 + 1 < 8**

> means the first number is larger than the second.   **6 − 2 > 1**

= means the two numbers are equal (the same).   **3 + 2 = 5**

04

Compare these changing **population** figures for two Chinese towns: Key: 👤 =100 people

YEAR	TOWN A	TOWN B	TOTAL
1900	👤👤👤👤👤👤👤👤👤	👤👤👤👤👤👤👤	👤👤👤👤👤👤👤👤👤👤👤👤👤👤👤👤
1950	👤👤👤👤👤👤👤👤	👤👤👤👤👤👤👤👤	👤👤👤👤👤👤👤👤👤👤👤👤👤👤👤👤
2000	👤👤👤👤👤👤👤👤👤👤	👤👤👤👤👤👤👤👤👤	👤👤👤👤👤👤👤👤👤👤👤👤👤👤👤👤👤👤👤

In 1900, Town A had 900 people and Town B had 700: **900 > 700**
In 1950, Town A had 800 people and Town B had 800: **800 = 800**
In 1950, the total population was 1,600 and in 2000 it was 1,900: **1,600 < 1,900**

>GO FIGURE!

You are studying a town in China which has kept records of its population for a long time. You have records of people who lived there permanently, and the floating population of people who drifted in and out.

Year	Permanent population	Floating population
2008	234,117	451
1721	268,712	2,312
1919	242,419	740
1602	251,991	5,708
1871	239,022	4,219

1 Was the total population of the town larger in 1871 or 2008?

2 When was the earliest data recorded?

3 Put the correct signs <, >, or = between these pairs of numbers:

242,419 __ 234,117
234,117 __ 239,022
251,991 __ 268,712

4 Write out in words the permanent population in 1602.

5 When did the most people live in the town, including floating and permanent populations?

6 In your notepad, list the records in order of total population, starting with the lowest first.

ERUPTING GEYSERS

Your next mission takes you to Iceland to record the eruptions of a geyser. A geyser is a natural hot spring that regularly shoots huge jets of boiling water into the air.

LEARN ABOUT IT
TALLIES AND FREQUENCY TABLES

Many types of data are recorded by counting or tallying. Keeping a tally **is easier than counting as you make a mark for each item or event you see.**

$\setminus$ = 1 $||||$ = 4 $\cancel{||||}$ = 5

Draw four lines for the first four items, then draw a line through that group for the fifth. This makes it easy to count up later:

This tally shows (2 x 5) + 3 = 13

If you record tallies in a frequency **table**, you can write the total number in the last column. For example, this table shows a tally of the number of days two team members have spent on your Icelandic expedition:

	Days spent on expedition	Frequency
Alice	‖‖ ‖‖ ‖‖ \	16
Gabriel	‖‖ ‖‖ ‖‖ ‖‖ \\	22

>GO FIGURE!

This first table shows the number of eruptions you recorded on each day this week:

	Eruption tally	Eruption frequency
Monday	卌 II	
Tuesday	IIII	
Wednesday	卌	
Thursday	III	
Friday	IIII	

This table shows the number of days that had a particular number of eruptions:

Number of days	Number of eruptions per day
2	6
3	4
4	3
5	2

1 In the first table, how many days had four eruptions?

2 Copy out the first table in your notepad and fill in the last column with the number of eruptions on each day.

3 Looking at the second table, how many days did your team take records for?

4 How many eruptions were recorded in the second table?

FOSSIL HUNTING

You have traveled to Mongolia where dinosaur fossils have been found. You have been asked to buy fossils for a museum back home.

LEARN ABOUT IT
WORKING WITH MONEY

Working with money is the same as working with any other decimal numbers.

Sometimes, you might have to work to a budget. This means there is a limited amount of money to spend. Aside from the fossils, you have $20 to spend on supplies for your trip. You have found some things you would like to buy:

If you add up all the numbers, these items come to $24.32, so you cannot afford to buy all of them. You need to reduce your bill by $4.32. You could put back the first aid kit and the tools, or just the water.

If you paid for the food and the water with a $20 bill, you would get $1.06 in change:

$20 − ($10.99 + $7.95) = $1.06 change

FOSSIL HUNTERS SUPPLIES
RECEIPT

FIRST AID KIT $2.40

FOOD.............................$10.99

WATER............................... $7.95

TOOLS $2.98

TOTAL **$24.32**

❯GO FIGURE!

This is the price list for the different fossils:

PRICE LIST

FOSSIL 1 $105.39

FOSSIL 2 $97.12

FOSSIL 3 $73.40

FOSSIL 4 $34.75

1. What is the difference in price between fossil number 1 and fossil number 2?

2. Which fossil is the cheapest?

3. You have $200. What is the largest number of fossils you can buy?

4. You decide to buy fossils 2 and 4. What are the prices of each, rounded to the nearest $10?

5. You pay for fossils 2 and 4 with seven $20 bills. How much change do you get?

TAKING FOSSILS HOME

You have bought some fossils and now you need to work out how much space they will take up on the flight home and how many boxes you will need to pack them.

LEARN ABOUT IT
CUBIC UNITS AND VOLUME

The volume **of a three-dimensional object is the amount of space it takes up. Volume is measured in cubic units, such as cubic meters (m³), or cubic centimeters (cm³).**

If you imagine a shape made up of **cubes** with sides that were one meter, you could work out the volume by counting the cubes.

The volume of each cube is worked out by multiplying the base x depth x height:

1 x 1 x 1 = 1 m³

This shape is made up of six cubes. It has two rows of three cubes:

**2 x 3 = 6 cubic units
Total volume = 6 m³**

The volume of this shape is three cubic units.

You can rearrange the cubes and the volume remains the same.

The volume of a shape is often used in other calculations. If each cube was a box that contained 12 fossils, you could work out the total number of fossils.

This shape contains 3 x 12 = 36 fossils.

>GO FIGURE!

All the fossils you have bought have been packed into boxes and piled up ready to be sent home. The volume of each box is 1 m³.

Check List

=1 m³

Number of cubes?

Book transportation ✓

Transportation cost
($2.12 per m³)

1. You need to book transportation for the boxes. What is the total volume of the boxes?

2. To transport the boxes costs $2.12 per m³. How much will it cost?

3. What would the stack of boxes look like if you stood in front of the short edge and looked at it? Draw a picture of it in your notepad.

4. Draw another arrangement of the boxes with the same volume.

GEMSTONES IN POMPEII

You are visiting the ancient Roman city of Pompeii, which was destroyed by a volcanic eruption of Mount Vesuvius in 79 CE. The records you discover there use **Roman numerals** instead of numbers.

LEARN ABOUT IT
ROMAN NUMERALS

The Romans did not use the number system we use. Instead, they used letters to represent numbers.

1	I
5	V
10	X
50	L
100	C
500	D
1,000	M

They combined letters to make numbers. Counting up to 3 is easy:

I, II, III

12

But they did not use more than three of the same letter in a row.

"4" is shown as "5 − 1": put the "I" before the "V" to show it is taken away:

4 = IV

Numbers over 5 use "V" and "I". Put the letter for the largest number first:

VI (5 + 1 = 6), VII (5 + 2 = 7), VIII (5 + 3 = 8)

Each time you get to three of the same letter in a row, it is time to use the "minus 1" method.

So "9" is "10 − 1" shown as "IX":

9 = IX (10 − 1 = 9)

Bigger numbers can get quite long. For example:

39 = XXXIX

XXX (for 30) + IX (10 – 1 = 9)

388 = CCCLXXXVIII

CCC (3 x 100) + L (50) + XXX (3 x 10) + V (5) + III (3 x 1)

These numbers show the pattern:

1, 2, 3	I, II, III	40	XL (= 50 – 10)
4	IV	50	L
5	V	60, 70, 80	LX, LXX, LXXX
6, 7, 8	VI, VII, VIII	90	XC (= 100 – 10)
9, 10	IX, X	99	XCIX (= 100 – 10 + 10 – 1)
11, 12, 13	XI, XII, XIII	100	C
14, 15	XIV, XV	201	CCI
19, 20	XIX, XX	437	CDXXXVII
30	XXX	500	D

›GO FIGURE!

You see a slate with the accounts of a Roman gem trader. The figures show how many gems the trader sold and how many he stocked.

ITEM	NUMBER STOCKED	NUMBER SOLD
DIAMONDS	XL	XXIX
EMERALDS	XCIV	
RUBIES	XXXVI	XXXVI
PEARLS	CCLV	

 1 How many pearls did the gem trader stock?

 2 How many diamonds were unsold?

 3 All the rubies sold, so the gem trader made

a note to buy twice as many on his next sales trip. What did he write down?

4 The gem trader did not fill in the column for emeralds that had

sold, but there was only 15 left in stock that were found in the ruins of the shop. How many had he sold? How would you write that in Roman numerals?

VOLCANIC THREAT

You have journeyed to Indonesia to study an active volcano. You need to take measurements and create a map of the region to **estimate** the damage that a volcanic eruption might cause.

LEARN ABOUT IT
SCALE DRAWING AND MULTIPLYING NUMBERS WITH ZEROS

14

A scale **drawing or map is an accurate image of a scene that has been drawn smaller or larger than real life.**

Maps are usually drawn to scale. You can use a ruler to measure a distance on scale maps and know exactly how far you have to travel. Scale drawings show the scale that has been used. To work out the real size or distance, multiply by the scale.

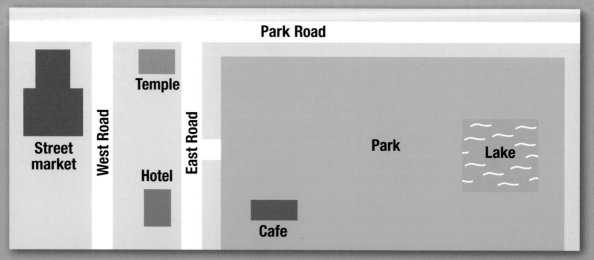

Park Road

Temple

West Road

East Road

Street market

Hotel

Park

Lake

Cafe

This map is at a scale of 1:10,000. Use your ruler to measure distances between objects on the map and then multiply by 10,000 to find out the real distance. For example, the lake is 2 cm wide, so in real life it is:

2 x 10,000 = 20,000 cm = 200 m

>GO FIGURE!

This map shows where the volcano is. You want to help the local people work out whether they will be in danger if the volcano erupts. Places up to 50 km away from the volcano are in danger.

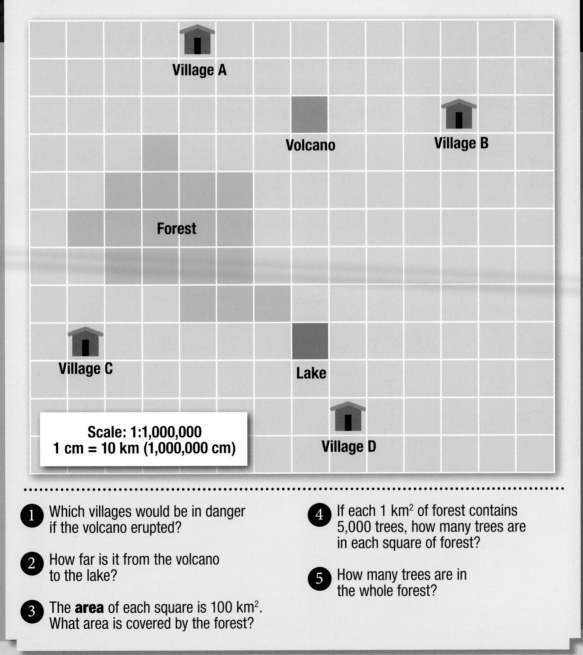

Village A

Volcano

Village B

Forest

Village C

Lake

Village D

Scale: 1:1,000,000
1 cm = 10 km (1,000,000 cm)

1 Which villages would be in danger if the volcano erupted?

2 How far is it from the volcano to the lake?

3 The **area** of each square is 100 km². What area is covered by the forest?

4 If each 1 km² of forest contains 5,000 trees, how many trees are in each square of forest?

5 How many trees are in the whole forest?

MELTING MOUNTAIN ICE

You have ventured to the chilly Himalaya Mountains to see how global warming is affecting the rate at which the glaciers are melting.

LEARN ABOUT IT
DIVISION

Division **helps you to work out shares or portions of numbers. You can think of division as taking one number away from another several times over.**

You can take 12 away from 48 four times, so $48 \div 12 = 4$:

$$48 - 12 = 36$$
$$36 - 12 = 24$$
$$24 - 12 = 12$$
$$12 - 12 = 0$$

Division is the opposite of multiplying.

$$48 \div 12 = 4 \text{ so } 4 \times 12 = 48$$

If you have a larger number, you need to break it down—for example, if you wanted to divide 2,520 by 7:

Write the numbers like this:

$$7 \overline{| 2520}$$

Try dividing the first digit by 7: $2 \div 7$ does not work.

Try with the first two digits: $25 \div 7$
$7 \times 3 = 21$, so 7 will go into 25 three times.

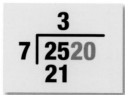

$$7 \overline{| 25\,20}$$ with 3 on top and 21 underneath

Put the "3" on top and the "21" underneath.

Show the subtraction to get the remainder: 25 – 21 = 4:

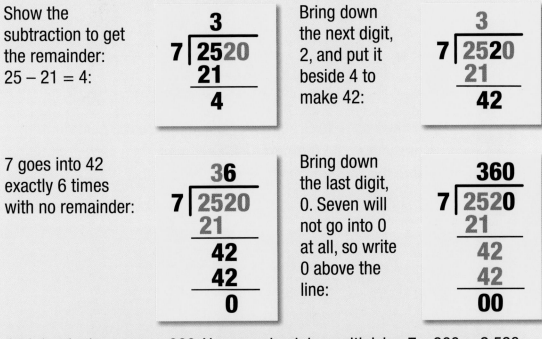

```
      3
   ┌────────
 7 │ 2520
   │ 21
   └────────
      4
```

Bring down the next digit, 2, and put it beside 4 to make 42:

```
      3
   ┌────────
 7 │ 2520
   │ 21
   └────────
      42
```

7 goes into 42 exactly 6 times with no remainder:

```
      36
   ┌────────
 7 │ 2520
   │ 21
   └────────
      42
      42
   ────────
      0
```

Bring down the last digit, 0. Seven will not go into 0 at all, so write 0 above the line:

```
      360
   ┌────────
 7 │ 2520
   │ 21
   └────────
      42
      42
   ────────
      00
```

And that is the answer: 360. You can check by multiplying 7 x 360 = 2,520.

›GO FIGURE!

During your time on the glacier, you estimate that about 43,740 liters of water will flow from the glacier in total.

1 If this volume of water melts over nine days, how many liters will flow each day?

2 You were given the wrong information. The volume of water melts over 90 days. How many liters of water flow each day?

3 Sixty households share the water from the glacier. How much water will each household have per day?

4 If the water flows too quickly, it floods the fields. To prevent this, it is divided between two channels. How much water flows through each channel every day?

5 If each channel was then used to water, or irrigate, three fields, how much water would each field receive per day?

FEELING COLDER

You have gone to Greenland to investigate the climate and, in particular, the temperature. Greenland is a very cold place where the temperature regularly falls below 0°C.

LEARN ABOUT IT
POSITIVE AND NEGATIVE NUMBERS

Negative numbers **are numbers that are less than zero.** Positive numbers **are numbers that are greater than zero.**

18

On a **number line**, the negative numbers are to the left of zero and the positive numbers are to the right of zero:

-10 -9 -8 -7 -6 -5 -4 -3 -2 -1 **0** 1 2 3 4 5 6 7 8 9 10

← negative numbers   positive numbers →

Some subtraction problems give an answer that is less than zero —a negative answer. If you take away 5 from 3, for example, the answer is -2. This is easy to see using a number line:

-10 -9 -8 -7 -6 -5 -4 -3 -2 -1 **0** 1 2 3 4 5 6 7 8 9 10

$3 - 5 = -2$

Numbers get smaller as you move to the left of the number line—
so -7 is a smaller number than -3. Numbers get larger as you
move to the right of the number line.

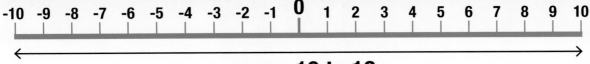

-10 -9 -8 -7 -6 -5 -4 -3 -2 -1 0 1 2 3 4 5 6 7 8 9 10

range -10 to 10

The range of this number line is 20, going from -10 to 10.

>GO FIGURE!

Because the temperature in Greenland gets very low, the
thermometer you are using shows mostly negative numbers.

-20 -19 -18 -17 -16 -15 -14 -13 -12 -11 -10 -9 -8 -7 -6 -5 -4 -3 -2 -1 0 1 2 3 4 5

1. The temperature now is 3°C. At night, it might go to -11°C. What is the difference in temperature?

2. Sometimes the temperature is less than -15°C. How many degrees below -15°C does the thermometer show?

3. Yesterday the temperature at different times of the day was: -8°C, -1°C, 4°C, -3°C. What was the highest temperature yesterday?

4. What was the lowest temperature yesterday?

5. What was the range of the temperatures recorded?

MONSOON TIME

You are in the Philippines during the monsoon, or rainy, season. Heavy rainfall is normal for this time of year.

LEARN ABOUT IT
PICTOGRAMS

A pictogram **is a chart that uses small pictures or icons to show a number of items or a measurement. It is easy to compare values with a pictogram.**

This pictogram uses pictures to show what the weather is like for each hour during a 24-hour period:

24-HOUR WEATHER FORECAST

12 am–8 am	☁ ☁ ☁ ☁ ☁ ○ ○ ○
8 am–4 pm	☁ ☁ 🌧 🌧 🌧 🌧 ○ ○
4 pm–12 am	○ ☁ ☁ ☁ ☁ ☁ ☁ ☁

From this, you can see that there were six hours of sunshine, four hours of rain and 14 hours of cloudy weather in total.

A pictogram is not a good way to show numbers exactly. If there were 40 minutes of sunshine, you might show $\frac{2}{3}$ of a Sun, but it would just look like more than half a Sun. When you draw your own pictograms, you need to choose carefully how to represent numbers. You need to show different things using different images, but too many could make the pictogram confusing.

>GO FIGURE!

Scientists at the research station you visit have kept a record of rainfall over the past few weeks. They have created a pictogram for you.

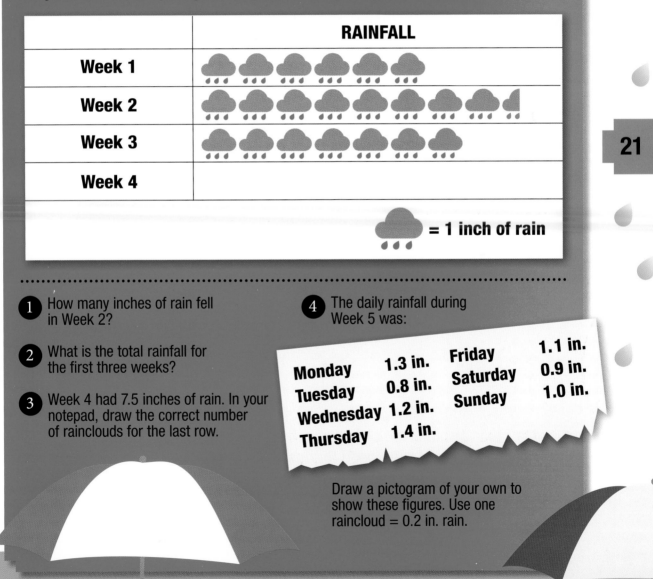

1 How many inches of rain fell in Week 2?

2 What is the total rainfall for the first three weeks?

3 Week 4 had 7.5 inches of rain. In your notepad, draw the correct number of rainclouds for the last row.

4 The daily rainfall during Week 5 was:

Monday	1.3 in.	Friday	1.1 in.
Tuesday	0.8 in.	Saturday	0.9 in.
Wednesday	1.2 in.	Sunday	1.0 in.
Thursday	1.4 in.		

Draw a pictogram of your own to show these figures. Use one raincloud = 0.2 in. rain.

SNOWED IN!

You are in Antarctica, but the weather is bad and you cannot leave. Your team has found various graphs and plots showing the predicted conditions in the area.

LEARN ABOUT IT
LINE PLOTS AND LINE GRAPHS

There are a lot of different types of graphs and charts. Some are more suitable for showing continuous data—figures taken from a constant stream of possible readings.

This line graph shows the size of an iceberg as it melts.

The iceberg does not shrink suddenly from one measurement to another, but shrinks slowly all the time. For example, by drawing a line up from June, you can estimate the size in that month. In this case it is 50 km^2.

Area = km^2

80
70
60
50
40
30
20
10
0

May   June   July   August   September   October

Date

Other types of charts are more suitable for showing separate amounts. **Line plots**, **bar graphs**, and **pie charts** are good for this type of data. This line plot shows how many icebergs were seen over three months.

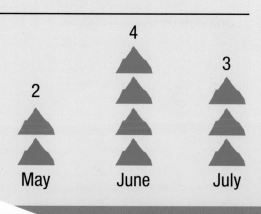

2
4
3

May   June   July

>GO FIGURE!

Your team has found a temperature graph as well as a line plot showing the number of icebergs that will be seen in the area.

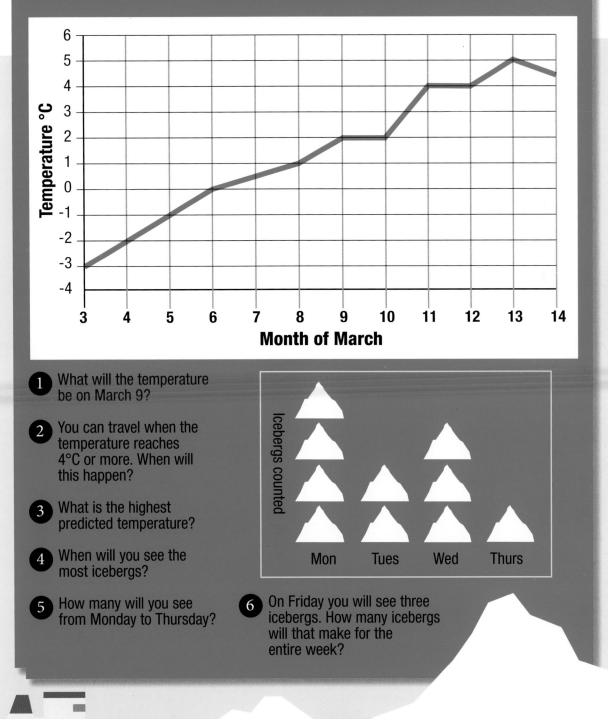

1. What will the temperature be on March 9?

2. You can travel when the temperature reaches 4°C or more. When will this happen?

3. What is the highest predicted temperature?

4. When will you see the most icebergs?

5. How many will you see from Monday to Thursday?

6. On Friday you will see three icebergs. How many icebergs will that make for the entire week?

DEEP-SEA DIVING

You have taken a submarine to see how the coral is growing on a tropical reef near Sydney, Australia. In particular, you are recording the shapes the coral grows in.

LEARN ABOUT IT
PLANE AND SOLID SHAPES

Flat, or plane shapes **are two-dimensional. The simplest plane shape is a** triangle, **which has three sides.**

triangle

Shapes with four sides are quadrilaterals. Those with four **right angles** are squares or **rectangles**. A square has four sides of the same length. A quadrilateral without right angles can be a parallelogram, a trapezium, or a rhombus.

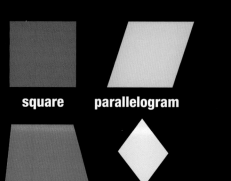

square   parallelogram

trapezium   rhombus

Here are some other shapes with more sides:

5 pentagon   6 hexagon   7 heptagon   8 octagon

A regular shape with a curved outline can be a circle or an ellipse.

circle   ellipse

Solid shapes are three-dimensional. Here are some regular solid shapes.

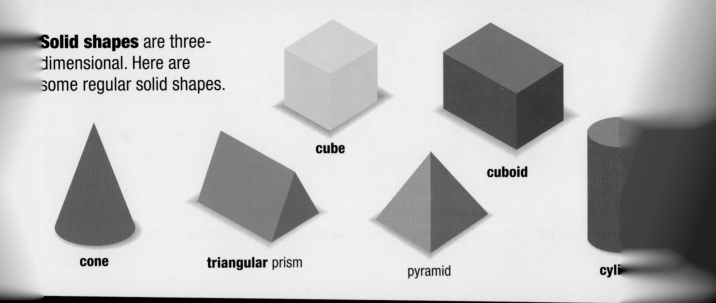

cube

cuboid

cone

triangular prism

pyramid

cyli

>GO FIGURE!

From your submarine, you check the coral shapes in two regions, or zones, of the coral reef.

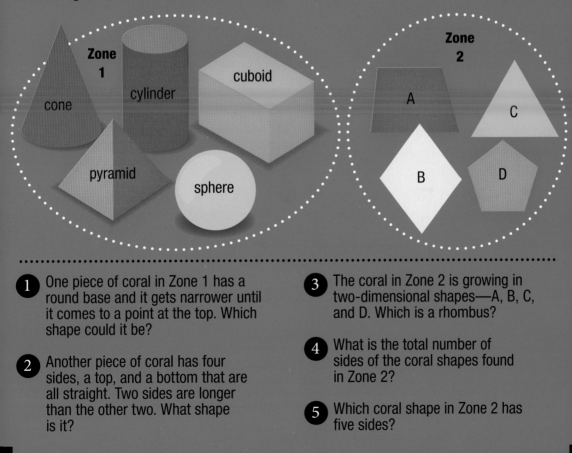

Zone 1

cone

cylinder

cuboid

pyramid

sphere

Zone 2

A

C

B

D

1 One piece of coral in Zone 1 has a round base and it gets narrower until it comes to a point at the top. Which shape could it be?

2 Another piece of coral has four sides, a top, and a bottom that are all straight. Two sides are longer than the other two. What shape is it?

3 The coral in Zone 2 is growing in two-dimensional shapes—A, B, C, and D. Which is a rhombus?

4 What is the total number of sides of the coral shapes found in Zone 2?

5 Which coral shape in Zone 2 has five sides?

GLOBAL TIME

Your trip is over and you are writing up your final notes. You need to work out some details of the journeys you made during your expedition around the world.

LEARN ABOUT IT
WORKING WITH TIME

We can tell the time using an analog **clock or a** digital **clock.**

26

A digital clock can work as a 12-hour clock or a 24-hour clock. A 12-hour clock shows numbers from 00:00 to 12:00 for both morning (am), and afternoon to evening (pm). A 24-hour clock numbers the hours from 00:00 to 24:00.

Analog clock (12-hr)
3:40 pm

Digital clock (24-hr)
15:40

The world is divided into time zones.

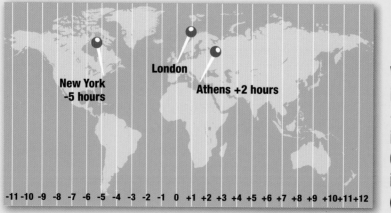

New York
-5 hours

London

Athens +2 hours

-11 -10 -9 -8 -7 -6 -5 -4 -3 -2 -1 0 +1 +2 +3 +4 +5 +6 +7 +8 +9 +10+11+12

When it is 12:00 in London, it is -5 hours (earlier) in New York, so 07:00. In Athens, it is +2 hours (later), so 14:00.

For example, you leave Athens at 10 am and it takes 5 hours to get to London. To find out the time in London when you arrive, you need to take away 2 hours (the time difference) and then you need to add 5 hours (the flight time).

LEAVE ATHENS		ARRIVE IN LONDON (+ 5 HOURS)	
Athens time	London time	**Athens time**	London time
10:00	08:00	**15:00**	13:00

>GO FIGURE!

You have plotted a map of the places you have visited, along with their time zones. Some countries choose their own time zones, and these might not be the same as other places in the region. For example, Iceland has the same time zone as London.

1. You arrived in Indonesia at 3 pm. What time was it in Pompeii?

2. You arrived in Sydney at 17:30 local time and phoned a friend in Chicago. What time was it in Chicago?

3. The distance from China to Iceland is nearly 8,000 km. If the plane flies at 800 km/h, how long will the flight last?

4. If your flight leaves China at 6 am, what is the time in Iceland when you arrive?

5. Your phone shows the time using the 24 hour clock—write down the local departure and arrival times for the China to Iceland flight.

ANSWERS

04-05 Around the world
1. 1871
2. 1602
3. 242,419 > 234,117
   234,117 < 239,022
   251,991 < 268,712
4. Two hundred and fifty-one thousand, nine hundred and ninety-one.
5. 1721
6.

Year	Total population
2008	234,568
1919	243,159
1871	243,241
1602	257,699
1721	271,024

06-07 Erupting geysers
1. Two days – Tuesday and Friday
2.

	Tally	Frequency
Monday	||||‖ ||	7
Tuesday	||||	4
Wednesday	||||‖	5
Thursday	|||	3
Friday	||||	4

3. 2 + 3 + 4 + 5 = 14 days
4. (2 x 6) + (3 x 4) + (4 x 3) + (5 x 2) = 12 + 12 + 12 + 10 = 46 eruptions

08-09 Fossil hunting
1. $105.39 – $97.12 = $8.27
2. Fossil 4
3. Two; the cheapest three all together cost $205.27
4. Fossil 2: $100; Fossil 4: $30
5. 7 x $20 = $140 to spend
   $97.12 + $34.75 = $131.87
   $140 – $131.87 = $8.13

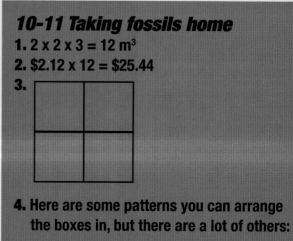

10-11 Taking fossils home
1. 2 x 2 x 3 = 12 m³
2. $2.12 x 12 = $25.44
3.
4. Here are some patterns you can arrange the boxes in, but there are a lot of others:

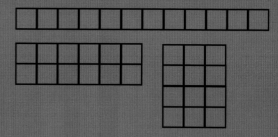

12-13 Gemstones in Pompeii
1. 255
2. 40 – 29 = 11
3. 2 x 36 = 72, so he wrote LXXII
4. He had 94; 94 – 15 = 79, which is LXXIX

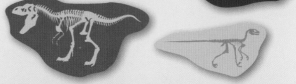

14-15 Volcanic threat
1. Villages A and B
2. The distance is 50 km

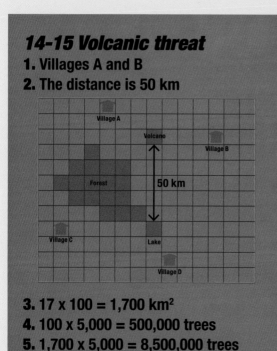

3. 17 x 100 = 1,700 km²
4. 100 x 5,000 = 500,000 trees
5. 1,700 x 5,000 = 8,500,000 trees

16-17 Melting mountain ice
1. 43,740 ÷ 9 = 4,860 liters per day
2. 43,740 ÷ 90 = 486 liters per day
3. 486 ÷ 60 = 8.1 liters per day
4. 486 ÷ 2 = 243 liters per day
5. 243 ÷ 3 = 81 liters per day

18-19 Feeling colder
1. The temperature difference between 3°C and -11°C is 14°C.
2. The thermometer goes down to -20°C. 20 – 15 = 5, so there are 5 more degrees shown below -15°C.
3. The highest temperature was 4°C.
4. The lowest temperature was -8°C.
5. The temperature range from 4°C to -8°C is 12°C.

20-21 Monsoon time
1. 8.5 inches
2. 6 + 8.5 + 7 = 21.5 inches
3.

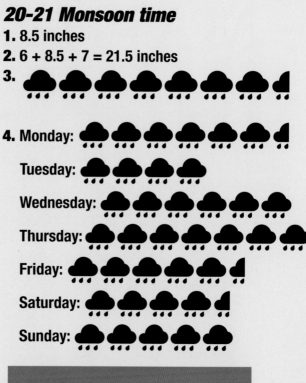

4. Monday:

Tuesday:

Wednesday:

Thursday:

Friday:

Saturday:

Sunday:

22-23 Snowed in!
1. 2°C
2. March 11
3. 5°C
4. Monday
5. 4 + 2 + 3 + 1 = 10
6. 10 + 3 = 13

24-25 Deep-sea diving
1. Cone
2. Cuboid
3. Coral B
4. 4 + 4 + 3 + 5 = 16 sides
5. D – it is a pentagon

26-27 Global time
1. 3 pm – 7 hours = 8 am
2. 17:30 – 16 hours = 01:30
3. 8,000 ÷ 800 = 10 hours
4. 6 am (time at start) + 10 hours (length of flight – 8 (time difference) = 8 am
5. Depart: 06:00, Arrive: 08:00

MATH GLOSSARY

ANALOG
An analog clock has a round face with numbers and hands to point out the time.

AREA
The amount of two-dimensional space covered by a shape or object. For example, the area of a rectangle is calculated by multiplying the length of one of the short sides by the length of one of the long sides.

BAR GRAPH
A type of chart that uses vertical bars to show the frequency of different pieces of data

CUBE
A three-dimensional shape that is formed from six square sides

DECIMAL
Dividing whole numbers into smaller units. One can be divided into ten decimals (tenths), and these can be divided into ten smaller decimals (hundredths), and so on.

DIGITAL
A digital clock only uses numbers to tell the time.

DIVISION
Breaking up a number into smaller parts or seeing how many times one number will go into another one

ESTIMATE
To produce an answer that is roughly equivalent to the correct answer. Estimating usually involves rounding up or down the numbers involved.

LINE PLOTS
Line plots show the size of different sets of data, using an "x" or some other symbol to show the frequency or size of each data set.

NEGATIVE NUMBER
A number that is less than zero

NUMBER LINE
A line that is divided into numbers and can be used to show a progression in increasing or decreasing values

PICTOGRAM
A chart that uses small images to represent numbers and information

PIE CHART
A type of chart that divides a circle into "slices" according to the proportion shown by each value. The bigger the value, the larger the slice on the pie chart.

PLANE SHAPE
A two-dimensional shape, such as a triangle or a square

POPULATION
The number of people who live in a particular area, such as a town, region, or country

POSITIVE NUMBER
A number that is greater than zero

PRISM
A three-dimensional shape that has two identical ends and flat sides. The shape of the ends determines the name of the prism, such as a triangular prism.

PYRAMID
A three-dimensional shape whose sides are formed from triangles that meet at a point above a base. The base can be a triangle, square, rectangle, or any shape with three or more sides.

RECTANGLE
A four-sided shape where two sides are longer than the other two and all four corners have an angle of 90°

RIGHT ANGLE
An angle of 90°

ROMAN NUMERALS
A system of counting used by the Romans which featured combinations of letters instead of numbers

1	I
5	V
10	X
50	L

SCALE
A number that shows how much a map or drawing has been made smaller. For example, a scale of 1:1,000, means that the image is 1,000 times smaller than the original, so 1 cm on the drawing represents 1,000 cm, or 10 m, in real life.

SOLID SHAPES
A three-dimensional shape, such as a cube or a sphere

TABLE
A way of laying out numbers and information in rows and columns

TALLY
A method of recording events or objects where a simple line is used to record each occurrence. Every fifth line is drawn across the previous four, creating easy-to-spot groups of five.

TRIANGLE
A shape with three sides. There are three types of triangle. An equilateral triangle has all three sides and angles the same. An isosceles has two of its sides and angles the same. A scalene triangle has all three sides and angles that are different.

VOLUME
The amount of space an object takes up. It is measured in cubic units, such as cubic centimeters (cm^3) or cubic meters (m^3).

LEARNING MORE

WEBSITES

www.mathisfun.com
A huge website packed full of explanations, examples, games, puzzles, activities, worksheets, and teacher resources for all age levels.

http://ca.ixl.com/math/grade-4
Practice your math skills by answering questions in various categories. The questions will automatically get harder as you improve!

www.mathplayground.com
An action-packed website with math games, mathematical word problems, worksheets, puzzles, and videos.

INDEX

analog clocks 26
area 15

bar charts 22

cubes 10, 11, 25
cubic units 10, 11

decimal numbers 8
digital clocks 26
distances 14, 15
division 16, 17

frequency tables 6, 7

large numbers 4, 5
line graphs 22, 23

line plots 22, 23

maps 14, 15, 26, 27
money 8, 9
multiplying 14, 16

negative numbers 18, 19

pictograms 20, 21
pie charts 22
plane shapes 24, 25
populations 4, 5
positive numbers 18, 19

quadrilaterals 24

rectangles 24

Roman numerals 12, 13

scale drawings 14, 15
solid shapes 25

tables 6, 7
tallies 6, 7
temperatures 18, 19
time zones 26, 27
triangles 24

volume 10, 11

zero 14, 18, 19

g°figure

+<=[A Math]~±÷
Journey Through
PLANET EARTH

Go on a mission to protect some of world's most threatened areas, and use your math skills to measure geysers, protect forests, and check glaciers. Math puzzles and exercises help you use the power of volume, scale, division, and number lines to explore our planet.

Titles in the series

+<=[A Math]~±÷ Journey Through the ANIMAL KINGDOM

+<=[A Math]~±÷ Journey Through the HUMAN BODY

+<=[A Math]~±÷ Journey Through PLANET EARTH

+<=[A Math]~±÷ Journey Through SPACE

Guided Reading: R

U.S.A. $9.95
Canada $10.95

CRABTREE
Publishing Company
www.crabtreebooks.com

ISBN 978-0-7787-0736-3

9 780778 707363

planet earth

BIG
WORLD,
SMALL
WORLD

SCHOLASTIC

planet earth

BIG
WORLD,
SMALL
WORLD

A Journey Through Earth,
from the Blue Whale to the Bullet Ant

By Kris Hirschmann

SCHOLASTIC INC.

New York   Toronto   London   Auckland   Sydney
Mexico City   New Delhi   Hong Kong   Buenos Aires

BBC (word mark and logo) are trade marks of the British Broadcasting Corporation and are used under licence.

Planet Earth logo © BBC 2006. BBC logo © BBC 1996. Love Earth logo TM BBC.

Published by Scholastic Inc. SCHOLASTIC and associated logos are trademarks and/or registered trademarks of Scholastic Inc.

ISBN-13: 978-0-545-11162-1
ISBN-10: 0-545-11162-5

12 11 10 9 8 7 6 5 4 3 2   9 10 11 12 13 14/0
Printed in the U.S.A.
Printed on paper containing minimum of 30% post-consumer fiber.
First printing, April 2009

contents

Section I: Pole to Pole 4

Section II: Mountains
Walia Ibex 10
Siberian Musk Deer 11
Giant Panda........................ 12
Red Panda........................... 13
Snow Leopard 14
Monal Pheasant................... 15

Section III: Ocean Deep
Blue Whale 16
Radiolarian.......................... 17
Whale Shark 18
Pilot Fish 19
Red Spider Crab.................. 20
Shrimp 21
Manta Ray 22
Panda Pteropod 23

Section IV: Deserts
Bactrian Camel.................... 24
Augrabies Flat Lizard............. 25
Red Kangaroo 26
Fennec Fox.......................... 27
Lion.................................... 28
Desert Locust 29

Section V: Ice Worlds
Emperor Penguin.................. 30
Adélie Penguin..................... 31
Walrus................................ 32
Little Auk............................ 33
Polar Bear........................... 34
Arctic Fox 35
Sandhill Crane 36
Snow Petrel 37

Section VI: Shallow Seas
Humpback Whale 38
Great White Shark 39
Sunflower Sea Star................ 40
Brittle Star.......................... 41
Coral Polyps 42
Purple Sea Urchin 43

Section VII: Great Plains
Asian Elephant..................... 44
Pygmy Hog 45
Ostrich 46
Red-Billed Quelea 47
Wild Yak 48
Pika 49

Section VIII: Jungles
Chimpanzee......................... 50
Emperor Tamarin 51
Bongo 52
Bullet Ant 53
Siamang Gibbon................... 54
Gliding Leaf Frog.................. 55

Section IX: Fresh Water
Nile Crocodile 56
Piranha 57
Nerpa................................. 58
Smooth-Coated Otter............. 59
Sockeye Salmon.................... 60
Cichlid................................ 61

Section X: Seasonal Forests
Moose................................ 62
Pudu 63
Lynx 64
Kodkod 65
Wolverine 66
Periodical Cicada 67

Section XI: Caves
Wrinkle-Lipped Bat................ 68
Belizean White Crab.............. 69
Cave Swiftlet 70
Cave Glowworm 71
Cave Centipede.................... 72
Cave Molly 73

Conclusion 74

Photo Credits........................... 77

pole to pole

Of all the planets in the solar system, Earth is the only one that can claim life. That wasn't always the case. In its earliest days, the Earth was nothing but a hot ball of molten rock. This volcanic activity released gases that formed a primitive atmosphere. Another result of this volcanic activity was water vapor — enough of it to form oceans. As the atmosphere thickened and the oceans grew, conditions became favorable for the creation of life.

Around 4 billion years ago, the incredible finally happened. Through an unknown process, simple living organisms appeared in the Earth's oceans. These organisms would evolve into the millions of species that roam our planet today.

pole to pole

Much of this evolution was shaped by a cosmic fender bender. Soon after the Earth formed, it bumped into a planet about the size of Mars. The impact threw as much as 70 percent of our planet's rocky crust into space. The remaining crust was so thin that it cracked into enormous plates. The plates' movements shoved mountains into the air and ripped apart wide trenches, creating many different living environments.

The collision also knocked the Earth partly onto its side. Our planet, which had once stood straight up and down on its axis, was now tilted at a 23-degree angle. The tilt has a huge effect on the Earth's climate. By changing the way sunlight reaches the Earth's surface, it causes our seasons as well as our wet and dry cycles.

AT A GLANCE

- Our solar system *was created* between **4.5 and 5 billion years ago.**

- The Earth *orbits the Sun* at a distance of **93 million miles** (149.6 million km). This distance seems to be ideal for the support of life.

- The *average surface temperature* of the Earth is **63 degrees** Fahrenheit (17 degrees Celcius).

- *All life on Earth* depends on two ingredients: **energy** from the Sun and **liquid water**.

pole to pole

Continental drift, seasons, and other factors came together to shape the planet we now know. It boasts wooded areas and the rivers that run through them, tropical rainforests and equally colorful shallow seas, wide-open grasslands and closed-in underworlds, the highest mountains and the deepest oceans.

Some of these habitats are kinder than others. Yet even the harshest environments have something to offer — and if there is any benefit to be had, an animal will learn how to take advantage of it. From the biggest to the smallest, these animals make up the tapestry of

mountains

Mountains are among our planet's most majestic natural features. But with their harsh conditions, mountains do not seem like a comfortable place to live. Yet they support a great deal of life, including some of the Earth's rarest animals.

Walia Ibex

Ethiopia's Simien Mountains are dotted with rocky spikes and canyons. The rough ground seems impossible to navigate. Yet one large animal, the walia ibex, does the job with ease. Thanks to its rubbery, rock-clinging hooves, this goat-relative keeps its footing.

Walia ibexes stick to the mountains for one very important reason: food. In the mountains, frequent rainfall helps grasses, herbs, and other tasty plants thrive. By living the high life, the walia ibex guarantees itself a never-ending supply of the food it needs to survive.

DID YOU KNOW?

The **Ethiopian Highlands**, where the Simien Mountains are found, are *Africa's largest land area* over 9,840 feet (3,000 m). For this reason, the area is sometimes called *"The Roof of Africa."*

Siberian Musk Deer

Like the walia ibex, the Siberian musk deer is an ungulate (hoofed animal). Compared to its super-sized relative, though, the musk deer comes up short. Adults of this species stand between 20 and 24 inches (51 and 61 cm) at the shoulder and weigh as little as 15 pounds (7 kg).

Musk deer are found in mountainous regions of China, Mongolia, Russia, North Korea, and South Korea. They live on steep, forested slopes, hiding during the day and coming out to forage at night. They feed mostly on lichens, which they nibble off tree trunks and branches.

DID YOU KNOW?

Male musk deer produce a *strong-smelling substance* called **musk**. The scent acts as a warning to other male deer: **"Stay away from my home!"**

Musk deer have **powerful hind legs**. Using these legs, *a musk deer can jump nearly 20 feet (6 m)* to escape from a hungry predator.

PLANET QUIZ

The Siberian musk deer is the only deer in the world to have which organ?

a) Appendix   b) Gall bladder

c) Liver   d) Adrenal gland

Answer: b) Gall bladder. This organ stores a substance called bile and helps in the digestive process.

Giant Panda

Weighing up to 275 pounds (125 kg), the giant panda of the eastern Himalayas is one of the world's best-loved animals. It's easy to see why. As a plant eater, this creature has a better temper and a calmer lifestyle than most bears. It moves gently through its high-altitude home, stopping often to munch on bamboo shoots.

Giant pandas need bamboo to survive, but this plant has few nutrients, so unlike many other bears, the panda must keep eating all year long. It never gets enough nutrients from the bamboo to hibernate.

DID YOU KNOW?

Bamboo has an unusual life cycle. Every 60 to 120 years, all the bamboos of a single species sprout flowers and create seeds. *Then they die, leaving the forest empty* for a new generation of bamboo plants to sprout. *This cycle can be a* **disaster** *for giant pandas.* If they cannot find another bamboo stand, they **go hungry**.

At birth, a panda cub weighs about **one-thousandth** of its mother's weight. *Newborn cubs are naked, blind, and toothless.*

Red Panda

Alongside the giant panda lives the red panda, a mountain bear about the size of a raccoon. Like giant pandas, these small animals must eat bamboo to survive. They prefer the plant's leaves and will gobble down up to 200,000 of them in a single day.

Because red pandas don't absorb much energy from their meals, they tend to sleep a lot. When awake, they move slowly and eat as much as they possibly can.

DID YOU KNOW?

The word **"panda"** comes from the Nepalese words *nigalya ponya*, meaning *"eater of bamboo."*

Snow Leopard

You'll need to climb the mountains of central Asia to glimpse the elusive snow leopard, the highest-living land predator on Earth. Averaging about 100 pounds (45 kg) in weight, these animals are smaller than common leopards. They look bigger, though, due to their long tails and thick coats. A long tail helps the animal to balance when it leaps between rocky outcroppings. Dense fur keeps the leopard warm.

The snow leopard's coat has another purpose. It blends into snowy surroundings, making the leopard very hard to see. Combined with slow, careful movements, this built-in camouflage helps snow leopards sneak up on their prey.

DID YOU KNOW?

Unlike other big cats, **snow leopards do not roar.** They do moan sometimes, though, *when they want to attract other leopards.*

Snow leopards prefer to hunt on cloudy or snowy days. *Bad weather makes it harder for prey to see a hungry leopard approaching.*

Monal Pheasant

Weighing about 4 to 5 pounds (1.8 to 2.3 kg), monal pheasants are much smaller than snow leopards. They are easier to spot, however, thanks to their brilliant bodies. Males of this species sport feathers of metallic green, blue, purple, and orange-brown.

These colors are good for attracting mates, but they attract predators as well. For this reason, monal pheasants tend to gather on ledges that are hard for hunters to reach. They leave their homes in groups to forage along the snowline for berries, insects, and other tasty treats.

DID YOU KNOW?

Female monal pheasants are much more drably colored than males. Their feathers are dull dark brown. Their only color is the **bright blue** that rings their eyes.

Monals are found at altitudes up to 14,000 feet (4,350 m). *They migrate up and down the mountain* as the seasons change and the snowline moves.

PLANET QUIZ

In scientific terms, strong physical differences between males and females of the same species are called:

a) Dimorphism   b) Bicoloration

c) Duoformality   d) Bifurcation

Answer: a) Dimorphism. Dimorphism is extremely common in the animal kingdom. It can include differences in size, color, or body parts.

15

ocean deep

In scientific terms, the deep sea is any place away from the Earth's coasts and beyond the continental shelves. This vast holding tank was once thought to be lifeless. But scientists now know that from their sunkissed surfaces to their deepest, darkest depths, the open oceans teem with life.

Blue Whale

Measuring up to 110 feet (33.5 m) from snout to tail and weighing in at a mighty 200 tons (181 metric tons), these marine mammals are thought to be the biggest animals ever to have lived on our planet.

Blue whales live in the vast open ocean, which makes them hard to find. However, the task is not impossible. From time to time they blast a mixture of air and water vapor out of blowholes on top of their heads. Rising up to 50 feet (15.3 m) above the surface, this "spout" leads scientists to their prodigious prey.

DID YOU KNOW?

Blue whales are the **world's loudest animals.** They can emit calls at levels *up to 188 decibels.* These sounds are **too low-pitched** for humans to hear. If you *could* hear them, though, *they would deafen you instantly.*

A blue whale's aorta (main artery) is wide enough for a *human being to crawl through.* **Its heart** is the size of a **small sports car**.

Radiolarian

Blue whales dine on plankton. Radiolarians are one type of plankton organism. Just one-tenth of a millimeter long, these tiny protozoa live in all of the world's oceans.

Radiolarians may be small, but they are of great importance to marine paleontologists. Dead radiolarians settle into ooze on the sea floor. This ooze eventually hardens into rock. Over millions of years, geologic processes may push the radiolarian rock into open air. The rocks serve as proof that oceans once covered the regions where mountains now stand.

PLANET QUIZ

Radiolarians are considered to belong to which family?

a) Animals   b) Plants

c) Fungi   d) None of the above

Answer: d) None of the above. Radiolarians have features of both plants and animals. They are usually called "protists" to separate them from these organisms.

Whale Shark

It might sound nuts to go swimming with a 46-foot (14-m) predator. But relax! You're in no danger around the whale shark, which is one of the ocean's gentlest giants. These animals feed on fish, plankton, krill, and squid.

Despite their name, whale sharks are not whales. They are true sharks — the biggest on Earth. These magnificent animals are found in warm seas around the world, from the surface to depths of about 2,500 feet (760 m). Always on the go, whale sharks cover huge distances in their never-ending search for food.

DID YOU KNOW?

Between May and July, **whale sharks** gather off the coast of Belize. *They feast on the roe of cubera snapper fish,* which spawn in huge numbers at this time of the year.

The **whale shark's flesh** *is eaten as food* in some countries, including Taiwan, Singapore, and Hong Kong.

DID YOU KNOW?

Pilot fish were once thought to lead, or pilot, larger fish to food sources. *This belief is the origin of the pilot fish's name.*

Pilot fish are found in the **open sea** throughout *warm and tropical waters.*

Pilot Fish

Whale sharks don't always swim alone. In the tropics, they often attract tagalong pals called pilot fish. Bearing bold black-and-blue stripes, these animals are usually about 14 inches (35 cm) long. They trail sharks of all species and other large predatory fish through the sea. Pilot fish know that the predators will eventually stop to eat. When they do, there will be plenty of scraps left over to feed a hungry hitchhiker.

PLANET QUIZ

Pilot fish and other animals that eat dead meat are called:

    a) Herbivores   b) Scavengers

    c) Detritivores   d) Decomposers

Answer: b) Scavengers. Scavengers play an important role in the ecosystem by helping to break down animals' remains.

ocean deep

Red Spider Crab

The Gulf of Mexico's blue-green waters look warm and inviting. Travel deep enough, however, and you will enter a pitch-black realm that sunlight cannot reach. This is the home of the red spider crab. Measuring more than 3 feet (1 m) across, these creatures crawl through the sea, using their claws to pluck dead fish and other food scraps off the ocean floor.

It might seem odd that a deep-sea creature would be so brightly colored, but without sunlight red objects appear black. So the red spider crab is perfectly camouflaged in its inky environment.

DID YOU KNOW?

Crabs *have ten legs*. The first two legs bear **pinching claws** called chela. The other eight legs are *used for walking* or, in some species, swimming.

A crab's shell **supports and protects** the soft parts of its body. It also limits the crab's size. *To grow, a crab must break out of its shell and form a new, larger one in a process called molting.*

Shrimp

Bottom-feeding crabs must fight many other creatures for every available scrap of food. In cold water, the biggest competition comes from pandalid shrimp, which measure anywhere from 1 to 4 inches (2.5 to 10 cm) in length.

All pandalids are born male. Around age two, they develop the ability to evolve into females. f the population is low, lots of males take this step. The new females lay thousands of eggs

Manta Ray

Manta rays are huge. Measuring up to 25 feet (7.6 m) across and weighing up to 2 tons (1.8 metric tons), manta rays can look quite scary. But like many of the ocean's giants, manta rays are filter feeders, not aggressive hunters. These creatures glide gently through the ocean, flapping their "wings" as they go.

DID YOU KNOW?

Manta ray pups are born wrapped up in their pectoral fins. *These fins grow to become the rays' wings.*

Manta rays sometimes **hurl their huge bodies** into the open air. *They fall back into the sea with a **massive splash** that dislodges parasites and loose, itchy skin.*

Panda Pteropod

Manta rays aren't the only underwater creatures that "fly." The feet of these snails have evolved into two see-through "wings." Pteropods flutter these wings to stay where they need to be in the water column.

Pteropods are very small, usually measuring less than half an inch (1 cm) in length. They have no way to defend themselves against predators. Luckily for the pteropod, nature has provided a built-in defense. These animals' bodies are almost transparent — and an animal that can't be seen is much less likely to be eaten.

PLANET QUIZ

Pteropods belong to a group called the gastropods. This word means:

    a) Foot-winged   b) Seed-eating
    c) Air-flled   d) Belly-footed

Answer: d) Belly-footed. This name comes from the fact that many gastropods crawl on their soft bellies, using them as "feet" to get around.

deserts

Deserts are among our planet's harshest places. Yet over millions of years, animals big and small have developed special features and tricks that equip them perfectly for their extreme desert homes.

Bactrian Camel

Big animals tend to be big drinkers. For this reason, the bone-dry Gobi desert seems like a bad home for such a large mammal. Yet the Bactrian camel manages to live comfortably in this environment. In the summer, these creatures hydrate their 1,400-pound (650 kg) bodies by eating water-rich plants. In the winter, a thirsty camel can gobble up to 2.5 gallons (11 l) of snow per day.

Bactrian camels are also among the only mammals on Earth that can drink salty water, which gives them the best possible chance of survival in the harsh desert.

DID YOU KNOW?

Bactrian camels *can survive extreme heat and cold, drought and famine, wind and snow.* They have **strong immune systems** that resist many common diseases.

A thirsty Bactrian camel can drink **25 gallons of water (110 l)** in five to ten minutes. Most large animals **would die** if they drank this much water, but *the Bactrian camel's body easily absorbs the liquid.*

Augrabies Flat Lizard

Like the Bactrian camel, the Augrabies flat lizard needs water to survive. But instead of searching for water, flat lizards spend their entire lives along a 50-mile (80-km) stretch of South Africa's Orange River in the Kalahari desert.

But the Orange River is not just a water source; it is a food source as well. Every day, blackflies hatch and emerge from the river. Groups of flat lizards gather on the

Red Kangaroo

Daytime temperatures in the Australian Outback could kill an unprotected human, but they are no problem for red kangaroos. These marsupials make their own cool spots by kicking away the soil's blistering upper layer. They rest their 200-pound (90-kg) bodies in these pits during the hottest hours.

Red kangaroos have another way to keep themselves from overheating. When things get really hot, kangaroos drool all over their fur. As the saliva evaporates, heat is drawn out of the blood vessels just beneath the surface and away from the body.

DID YOU KNOW?

Male kangaroos fight by kicking each

Fennec Fox

Like the red kangaroo, the fennec fox is built to endure heat. Found in the deserts of northern Africa, these animals weigh less than 3 pounds (1.4 kg). But compared to their body size, they have the largest ears of any fox on Earth. As blood flows through the ears, it radiates heat away from the fox's body.

Despite their built-in air conditioners, fennec foxes stay out of the sun as much as possible. These creatures dig burrows in the sandy desert soil. After the sun sets, they emerge to hunt.

DID YOU KNOW?

Fennec foxes are the smallest canids (dog relatives) on Earth. *Their bodies measure just 14 to 16 inches (36 to 41 cm) in length.*

Although fennec foxes *drink water,* studies suggest that they **do not need** to do it — **ever**. Fennecs are specially adapted to get *all of the moisture they need* through diet alone.

PLANET QUIZ

Which of the following adjectives does *not* describe a fox species?

a) Bat-eared   b) Crab-eating

c) Swift   d) Timber

Answer: d) Timber. There are bat-eared foxes, crab-eating foxes, and swift foxes, but no timber foxes.

deserts

Lion

In the desert, it is tough for a large predator to survive. But the Namib lions prove every day that it can be done. These creatures have smaller prides than other lion populations, so they don't need as much food to keep their family units fed.

An antelope called an oryx is the staple of the Namib lions' diet. Lions catch these animals by sneaking up on them. If a lion or lioness gets close enough, it rushes at the prey and wrestles it to the ground. When this task is complete, the entire pride settles in for a feast.

DID YOU KNOW?

Lions are sometimes called *"Kings of the Jungle."* This is an odd nickname, since lions are found in **just about every habitat** *except* jungles!

Lions prey on zebra, antelope, buffalo, oryx, and just about any other animals they can find. They will also **steal prey** from other predators or feed on carcasses.

In 1988, **a swarm of locusts** traveled from West Africa to the Caribbean. *The swarm covered a distance of more than 3,000 miles (4,825 km) in 10 days.*

A swarm of locusts **cannot be stopped.** It will keep moving *until it runs out of food and starves,* or rides wind currents out to the **open sea**.

Locusts can eat the equivalent of their own body weight in one day.

Desert Locust

The lion can't come close to matching the appetite of the desert locust. Common in Africa, the Middle East, and Asia, these grasshoppers are sparse most of the time. When conditions are right, however, billions of these creatures hatch at once. Locusts only measure 3 inches (7.5 cm) from head to tail. It seems impossible that such a small creature could be so destructive, but they eat until they have devoured every scrap of plant matter they can find. When the food is gone, the swarm takes to the sky in search of a new meal.

PLANET QUIZ

A charging lion can run how fast for short distances?

a) 25 mph (40 kph)   b) 35 mph (56 kph)

c) 45 mph (72 kph)   d) 55 mph (88 kph)

Answer: b) 35 mph (56 kph). Much of the lion's prey runs faster than this. To have any hope of success, lions must get very close to speedy prey before charging.

ice worlds

The polar regions are without question the world's least inviting spots. These species that live there are some of the toughest animals anywhere on the planet. That's what it takes to survive in an ice world, where staying fed and warm is the difference between life ... and death.

Emperor Penguin

Along the Antarctic coast lives the emperor penguin, the largest penguin species on Earth. These big birds can weigh up to 88 pounds (40 kg). About one-third of this weight consists of a thick layer of fat that is an emergency food source and a warm winter coat all in one.

That fur comes in handy especially for males. After the mating season, females head for the sea to hunt for food. Adult males stay, each balancing a single precious egg on his feet, keeping it warm under their bellies. They will not eat or drink until their mates return in two months' time. At this point, the males will have lost up to half of their body weight.

DID YOU KNOW?

Female emperor penguins *walk up to 100 miles (160 km)* to reach their colonies after they **return from the sea.**

At the end of the summer, *emperor penguins* are **too fat to sink** *easily in the water. They may swallow stones* to help them dive *longer and deeper.*

Adélie Penguin

Compared to its emperor cousin, the Adélie penguin is a real lightweight. This Antarctic bird tips the scales at about 9 pounds (4 kg). Although much of this weight is blubber, the Adélie simply doesn't have enough padding to withstand the Antarctic winter. It spends the coldest months of the year at sea.

When spring arrives, Adélie penguins head back south. They leap onto the still-frozen sea ice and slide their way to the rocky beaches where they will lay their eggs and bring a new generation into the world.

PLANET QUIZ

Traveling by sliding on the belly, as Adélie penguins do, is known as:

a) Tobogganing   b) Sledding

c) Snowboarding   d) Ice skating

Answer: a) Tobogganing. Adélie penguins can also walk and run, but tobogganing is their quickest way of getting around.

ice worlds

Walrus

On land, walruses are among the Earth's most awkward creatures, and it's no wonder. These massive animals can weigh as much as 4,000 pounds (1,815 kg). Between their tubby bodies and flipperlike legs, walruses struggle to heave themselves to the water's edge.

Everything changes, however, when a walrus finally plops into the sea. The water supports the walrus's bulk — and like magic, the walrus glides gracefully through the ocean, hunting for a meal to nourish its enormous body.

Little Auk

Measuring just 6 to 7 inches (15 to 18 cm) in length, Little Auks are designed for life on the sea and seem most comfortable when they are floating or swimming. In the water, in fact, they look and act a lot like mini penguins.

However, little auks have a skill that penguins have lost. Out of the water, they can spread their wings and take to the air. The Arctic is home to many predators. Flight is therefore a life-saving skill for the little auks.

DID YOU KNOW?

Little auks flap their wings very quickly *as they fly*. This movement creates a whiring sound that is very *distinctive*.

To **keep themselves safe** from larger birds, little auks travel in *gigantic flocks*. They leave and return to their colonies in **thousands-strong** swarms.

PLANET QUIZ

The word "vibrissae" refers to a walrus's:

a) Tusks   b) Flippers

c) Whiskers   d) Rolls of fat

Answer: c) Whiskers. Walruses have up to 700 of these appendages, which they use as feelers when hunting along the sea floor.

ice worlds

Polar Bear

Along the edges of the Arctic ice sheet lives the polar bear, the world's largest land carnivore. The biggest polar bears can grow up to lengths of 8 feet (2.5 m) and weights of 1,600 pounds (720 kg).

The fall and winter months are prime hunting times for polar bears. They go on an eating frenzy, ambushing seals when they swim to the water's surface to breathe.

When spring arrives, the polar bear must take to the sea, paddling from ice floe to ice floe in search of prey.

DID YOU KNOW?

Under all that **white fur**, *polar bears have black skin*. Dark colors absorb heat better than light ones, so a polar bear's dark skin helps it to **stay warm**.

Hungry polar bears *have been known to attack walruses and beluga whales.*

Arctic Fox

Another predator, the Arctic fox, roams the same areas as the polar bear. Competition? Hardly. Measuring just 18 to 27 inches (46 to 68 cm) in length and weighing as little as 6.5 pounds (3 kg), these animals stick to small prey.

Unlike polar bears, Arctic foxes thrive during the summer. They gorge themselves on the many birds and rodents that breed on the Arctic mainland. In wintertime, however, Arctic foxes have a much harder time. They sometimes follow polar bears, hoping to snag a few leftover scraps from the bigger predator's meal.

PLANET QUIZ

Polar bears use their claws for:

a) Traction on the ice

b) Digging through ice sheets

c) Killing prey

d) All of the above

Answer: d) All of the above. Strong and sharp, the polar bear's claws are very important survival tools.

Sandhill Crane

Sandhill cranes are hard to miss. These big birds stand nearly 4 feet (122 cm) tall and have up to 6-foot (183-cm) wingspans.

In warm regions, they are most common during the winter months. They spend this time in meadows and marshes, feeding on small animals, grain, and grass shoots.

When spring arrives, sandhill cranes take flight. They head north to their Arctic breeding grounds. The cranes nest on the grassy tundra, where predators are less likely to snatch their eggs or their newborn chicks. The big birds will stay in the Arctic until fall arrives. Then they will start the long return journey to their warm winter homes.

DID YOU KNOW?

Sandhill cranes refuse to put up with *predatory birds*. They **fly straight** at these animals, *kicking karate-style with their clawed feet.*

When courting, sandhill cranes *stretch their wings, pump their heads, leap into the air,* and **"dance"** in other ways to *impress possible mates.*

Snow Petrel

While the sandhill crane migrates halfway around the planet, the snow petrel stays put. Just 14 inches (36 cm) long, these birds seem too delicate to brave the Antarctic's worst weather — yet they roost along the edges of the ice pack all winter long.

When spring arrives, snow petrels head inland. They fly up to 215 miles (345 km) to build nests in bare, rocky cliffs. A female snow petrel will incubate a single white egg until it hatches. Then she and her mate will take turns making the 600-mile (965-km) round trip to the ocean to fetch food.

DID YOU KNOW?

The **snow petrel** is one of only three bird species that *breeds exclusively in Antarctica*.

Snow petrels **sometimes rub their feathers** in the snow to *clean themselves*.

PLANET QUIZ

True or false?

Snow petrels are highly endangered.

Answer: False. Snow petrel populations are considered healthy. They are covered by the 2001 Agreement on the Conservation of Albatrosses and Petrels, which requires nations to protect breeding colonies.

shallow seas

Continents do not end at the ocean's edge. They stretch outward underwater, forming shallow regions called continental shelves. This region is full of creatures that are very different from each other, but they all have something in common. They are perfectly suited for life in the coastal waters of Planet Earth.

DID YOU KNOW?

Humpback whales can fling their huge bodies *almost all the way out of the water*. This behavior is called **breaching**.

Humpbacks have the **longest pectoral fins** of any whale. *These immense "wings" are about a third as long as the whale's entire body.*

Humpback Whale

During winter, the world's warm seas come alive with humpback whales. These 50-foot (15.25-m) marine mammals have to travel from their summer homes near the Earth's poles. They need a safe place to breed, and shallow tropical waters provide the perfect nursery.

What they do *not* provide, however, is food. Humpback whales feed on krill, which are common in cold water but rare in warmer seas. Luckily, these huge animals can live off their stored fat until they return to their summer feeding grounds.

Great White Shark

The great white shark is one of the world's fiercest predators and biggest eaters. Growing up to 20 feet (6.1 m) long and weighing as much as 7,300 pounds (3,300 kg), these animals rip into fish, seals, dolphins, and anything else they can find.

Besides sheer bulk, there is another reason great whites are so powerful. This shark can keep its body 27 degrees Fahrenheit (15 degrees C) hotter than the surrounding water. The raised body temperature keeps the shark's senses sharp and gives the shark the energy to catch fast-moving prey.

DID YOU KNOW?

Great white sharks sometimes *lift their heads out of the water* to look for prey. They are **the only fish** known to do this.

PLANET QUIZ

Great white sharks are found mostly in:

a) Polar seas   b) Temperate seas

c) Subtropical seas   d) Tropical seas

Answer: b) Temperate seas. Great white sharks thrive in cool water. They are most common off the coasts of California, New England, Chile, Southern Africa, Australia, and New Zealand.

shallow seas

Sunflower Sea Star

DID YOU KNOW?

To **eat prey** bigger than itself, *a sunstar pushes its stomach out of its body.* It **wraps the stomach** around the prey and **digests** the unlucky animal *without ever swallowing it.*

Sunstars can **taste with their feet.** This means they can tell *whether an animal is tasty* just by stepping on it!

If bigger is better, then the sunflower sea star of the U.S. Pacific Coast is surely one of the ocean's most magnificent bottom dwellers. Also called sunstars, these creatures measure up to 39 inches (99 cm) across.

As if that weren't impressive enough, sunstars travel at lightning speeds compared to other sea stars. These animals can cover more than 40 inches (1 m) in a single minute. That may seem slow, but it's more than fast enough to overtake snails, sea urchins, and other sea-floor residents. Sunstars chase these animals, grab them, and gobble them down to sustain their hefty bodies.

Brittle Star

With central discs just 1/2 inch (1.3 cm) across, brittle stars make perfect snacks for sunstars — and they know it. So when a sunstar approaches, brittle stars flee. They use their long, thin arms to pull themselves out of harm's way.

When the danger has passed, brittle stars themselves become hunters. They bury themselves in the sandy seafloor, leaving an arm free to catch floating food particles or small animals.

PLANET QUIZ

Which group of animals is *not* related to sea stars and brittle stars?

a) Sea urchins   b) Feather stars

c) Octopuses   d) Sea cucumbers

Answer: c) Octopuses. Octopuses are mollusks. Sea stars, brittle stars, sea urchins, feather stars, and sea cucumbers are all classified as echinoderms, which means "spiny skin."

41

shallow seas

Coral Polyps

Australia's Great Barrier Reef is big enough to be seen from outer space. Yet this massive structure was built by one of the ocean's smallest creatures: the coral polyp. Just a few millimeters long, these animals cement themselves to hard surfaces soon after they hatch. Over thousands of years, the layers build up to form reefs that can stretch the length of an entire continent.

There are more than 2,000 coral species. These creatures need warmth and sunlight to survive, so coral reefs form only in the world's shallowest, most sun-drenched seas.

DID YOU KNOW?

There are **three types of coral reefs**. *Fringing reefs run in narrow bands* close to a coastline. **Barrier reefs** follow the coastline but tend to be far offshore. *Atolls are islands* that feature **rings of coral** around a central lagoon.

Certain algae live inside coral polyps' bodies. *The algae create waste products that act as food for the host polyp.*

Purple Sea Urchin

While corals are known for their building skills, the purple sea urchin is famous for the opposite reason: It has amazing destructive powers. Measuring just 2 to 4 inches (5 to 10 cm) across, these spiky animals crawl in hordes onto kelp stalks, chewing away the plant's base. The rest of the stalk floats to the surface and dies.

One kelp stalk might not seem like a big loss, but purple sea urchins can gather by the millions. Over time, they can mow down vast kelp forests — one bite at a time.

great plains

Animals of all sorts swarm to these waving fields of vegetation. Some are looking for hiding or nesting places and others are looking to feed on grass-munching prey. From the smallest insects and field mice to the largest grazers and predators, there is room for many creatures on the great plains of Planet Earth.

Asian Elephant

Asian elephants can grow up to 12 feet (3.7 m) and can weigh as much as 11,900 pounds (5,400 kg). With this much bulk, adult elephants are safe from most predators. Young elephants, however, are smaller and more vulnerable. Tall grasses shelter the offspring, keeping them from being noticed and possibly attacked.

DID YOU KNOW?

Adult male elephants go through periods called *musth*. During these times, often in winter, the elephant's **hormone levels** are *60 times greater than normal*. Elephants in musth are very **irritable**. They will even **attack other elephants** *if they come too close.*

Elephants sometimes **suck water into their trunks,** then *spray it onto themselves in a cooling shower.*

Pygmy Hog

The Indian grasslands also provide a home for smaller creatures, including the pygmy hog. Just 21 inches (53 cm) long and 7 to 11 inches (18 to 28 cm) in height, these little animals look like miniature wild boars.

A small body does not hold as much heat as a large one. Pygmy hogs struggle to stay warm when temperatures drop. They solve this problem by building grassy nests for themselves and their families. During periods of cold weather, mother hogs and their offspring snuggle together in these cozy beds.

PLANET QUIZ

By weight, a wild boar is about how many times larger than its pygmy hog cousin?

a) 10 times   b) 20 times

c) 30 times   d) 40 times

Answer: a) 10 times. The average weight of a pygmy hog is about 19 pounds (8.5 kg). Wild boars can weigh up to 198 pounds (90 kg).

great plains

Ostrich

On Africa's large, open plains, running is necessary for survival. One particularly fast species is the ostrich. This 8-foot (2.4-m), 300-pound (136-kg) bird has been clocked at speeds of 45 miles per hour (72 kph).

Should an ostrich get caught, it will use its powerful legs to kick at the attacker. Each of the ostrich's feet bears a long, curved claw. These claws can tear open a predator's soft belly — and save the ostrich's life in the process.

DID YOU KNOW?

Ostriches were once thought to bury their heads in the sand. *Scientists now know that this is not true.* Ostriches do, however, **lay their long necks flat on the ground** when they *don't want to be seen.*

Ostrich **eggs** are about *6 inches (15 cm) long and weigh about 3 pounds (1.4 kg) each* — the equivalent of **24 chicken eggs.**

Red-Billed Quelea

Sharing parts of the ostrich's range, these 5-inch (12.5-cm) birds can be seen in vast flocks throughout sub-Saharan Africa. In flight, a red-billed quelea flock is so thick that it is sometimes mistaken for locusts on the wing.

Unfortunately for African farmers, queleas don't just look like locusts. They act like them, too. Queleas tend to build colonies in farm areas and feed greedily in nearby fields. When they have gobbled down every bit of food in the surrounding area, they abandon their colonies and find new fields where they can satisfy their enormous appetites.

DID YOU KNOW?

Queleas nest in thorn bushes and trees. *Their colonies can cover up to 4 square miles (10.4 square kilometers).*

There were **not always so many** queleas in Africa. In recent decades, **large-scale human farming** *has led to a quelea population explosion.*

PLANET QUIZ

True or false?

Ostriches are the world's largest birds.

Answer: True. These animals are bigger than their closest relatives, the emus of Australia and the rheas of South America.

g eat plains

Wild Yak

Most animals couldn't get enough oxygen at the height of the Tibetan plateau, but the 2,200-pound (1000-kg) wild yak is specially adapted to life on the high plains. These animals have enormous lungs packed with blood vessels that absorb oxygen and carry it to all parts of the yak's body.

These creatures must also survive winter temperatures that drop to -40 degrees Fahrenheit (-40 degrees C). To manage this task, yaks are covered with hair so long that it nearly touches the ground.

DID YOU KNOW?

Wild yaks often attack domesticated yaks. *Animal experts are not sure why they do this.*

The wild yak's **skin** gives off a **goo** that acts *like hair gel*. By matting the yak's underhair, this **sticky substance** provides an *extra layer of protection against the cold.*

Pika

The 6-inch (15-cm) pika also braves the harsh winter of the Himalayan plains. Unlike yaks, though, these little rodents dig cozy burrows instead.

Many small animals hibernate when food is hard to find. Pikas, however, have a different strategy. During the fall, pikas gather grasses, seeds, nuts, and other foods. Then they carry these back to their burrows, where they arrange them in stacks called haypiles. The haypiles store all the food a pika needs to survive until spring.

DID YOU KNOW?

Pikas look like hamsters, but they are actually *related to rabbits*.

Pikas are found in *Alaska, Canada, Russia, and Japan* as well as in the **Himalaya Mountains**.

PLANET QUIZ

True or false?

Pikas use their tails to help them balance when hopping from rock to rock.

Answer: False. Pikas are almost tailless, but they seem to manage just fine without this tool.

jungles

Though rainforests only cover 3% of Earth's surface, they are home to half its species! The variety of life in the rainforest may be mind-bogglingly impressive, but it's not especially surprising. From the smallest to the biggest, rainforest species enjoy the most nurturing ecosystem on Planet Earth.

Chimpanzee

In the rainforests of Africa, chimpanzees, which can measure up to 5.5 feet (1.7 m) tall on their hind legs and weigh up to 150 pounds (68 kg), form communities that include dozens of individuals. They are friendly and social to their groupmates, but when they come into conflict with other chimp groups, they will band together and fight.

Chimpanzees are the ultimate omnivores. They use their intelligence to exploit almost every source of food — even insects! Chimps have even learned to make tools to help them dip into termite mounds for a tasty treat. Yummy!

DID YOU KNOW?

Chimpanzees are known to use *13 different plants as medicines.* Local people use many of the **same plants** *for headaches, infections, and stomach upsets.*

Chimps seem to be **fascinated** by snakes, especially pythons. *Groups of chimps sometimes surround a python and gaze curiously at it for 30 minutes or more.*

Emperor Tamarin

At just 9 inches (23 cm) in length and 1 pound (450 g) in weight, the emperor tamarin of Brazil and Peru is tiny compared to its African cousin, the chimp. But when it comes to food, tamarins and chimps have similar tastes. Tamarins love fruit and have a strong preference for figs.

Unlike chimpanzees, emperor tamarins do not compete for food. They cooperate instead. Groups of these monkeys sometimes travel with saddleback tamarins, a related species that eats the same foods. They call loudly to warn each other when predators approach.

PLANET QUIZ

When fruit is scarce, emperor tamarins eat mostly:

a) Insects   b) Nectar

c) Snails   d) Tree sap

Answer: b) Nectar. Although emperor tamarins do eat insects, snails, and tree sap, nectar makes up most of these animals' diets during the annual dry season.

jungles

Bongo

Standing about 50 inches (1.3 m) at the shoulder and weighing up to 900 pounds (410 kg), the bongo is the world's largest forest antelope. These boldly striped animals are found in Africa's Congo Basin and the rainforests of West Africa. Despite their size, bongos are not seen very often.

There is a good reason bongos are so careful. They are hunted by many powerful predators. Their best defense against these creatures is staying hidden. If this approach fails, bongos will protect themselves with their long, sharp horns.

Bullet Ant

Bongos are not the only animals with built-in weapons. The bullet ants of the Amazon rainforest have their own natural defense. The abdomens of these 1-inch (2.5-cm) insects contain long stingers that inject a toxin into prey or enemies.

There is little the bullet ant can do, however, to stop its most feared predator: the Cordyceps fungus. This fungus eats the internal organs, then it moves on to the brain. When the ant finally dies, the fungus sends stalks out of the corpse. Spores will float away from the stalks and infect any other ants that happen to be nearby.

jungles

Siamang Gibbon

At daybreak, the rainforests of Malaysia, Thailand, and Sumatra echo with the calls of the siamang, the largest member of the gibbon family. These 35-inch-tall (88-cm) apes often vocalize in groups. When they do, they produce songs that are surprisingly tuneful and complex.

If they're not singing, siamangs are probably swinging. These animals use their strong arms to swing through the treetops in search of tasty leaves, fruit, and flowers.

DID YOU KNOW?

Siamangs sing partly as a warning to other siamang families. *They are advertising their location and telling other apes to keep their distance.*

Although siamangs **can walk** on the ground, they *almost never do*. They spend nearly all of their time in trees at **heights of 80 to 100 feet** (24.4 to 30.5 m).

Gliding Leaf Frog

With a body around 3 inches (8 cm) long, the gliding leaf frog of the Central American rainforests can't match the power or the volume of the siamang. But that doesn't stop it from trying. After rain, males of this species gather in large groups around pools of water. Hundreds of tiny throats work together to make a noise much louder than a single leaf frog could manage.

The males' calls carry through the rainforest. They quickly catch the attention of females, who climb, jump, and glide through the trees, racing to find the loudest male, who is probably the biggest, strongest breeding partner as well.

DID YOU KNOW?

When leaping **from branch to branch**, leaf frogs spread their hands and feet wide. *The flaps in between create a parachute effect that lets the frog glide long distances.*

Most frog eggs need water. Gliding leaf frogs, however, lay their eggs on leaves. *The rainforest is so damp that the eggs can survive in the open air.*

PLANET QUIZ

Newly hatched frogs are called:

a) Larvae   b) Hatchlings

c) Tadpoles   d) Fry

Answer: c) Tadpoles. Tadpoles look like small fish. They live underwater until they grow limbs and lose their tails. Then they emerge to start their lives as adult frogs.

fresh water

Over millions of years, water can gouge canyons through solid rock. It can rearrange landscapes by carrying soil from one place to another. Fresh water also has a great effect on how animals live. The effect is biggest, of course, on creatures that live right in the water. Big, small, and in between, these animals spend their lives in or on Earth's most precious resource.

Nile Crocodile

The inland waters of southern Africa and Madagascar are home to hundreds of thousands of Nile crocodiles. These 16-foot (4.9-m), 2,500-pound (1,135-kg) animals rest along riverbanks, in marshes, and in mangrove swamps. They look too massive to move — but Nile crocodiles can run toward prey at speeds of 8.5 miles per hour (13.7 kph).

Once a crocodile has caught an animal, it doesn't let go. It clamps its huge jaws around its victim and tugs, tugs, tugs it toward the water's edge. The panicked prey is eventually pulled into deep water, where it is drowned and eaten by its toothy attacker.

Piranha

Predators don't have to be big to be dangerous. Need proof? Look no further than the red-bellied piranha of South America. Reaching a maximum length of about 13 inches (33 cm), these freshwater fish are ferocious hunters.

In the movies, piranhas are sometimes shown reducing large animals to skeletons within minutes. The images are terrifying — and highly exaggerated. Piranhas almost never target big, healthy creatures.

PLANET QUIZ

A group of birds is a flock; a group of elephants is a herd; and a group of crocodiles is a:

a) Purse   b) Skid

c) Chomp   d) Bask

Answer: d) Bask. This term actually refers to a group of crocodiles on land. In the water, crocodile groups are known as floats.

fresh water

Nerpa

Found in Siberia's Lake Baikal, nerpas are the region's only water mammals. These seals grow up to 4.6 feet (1.4 m) in length and can weigh up to 320 pounds (145 kg).

Nerpas depend heavily on another Lake Baikal resident: the golomyanka, also known as the oil fish. These fishes' bodies are about 35 percent oil by weight. They provide a high-calorie food source for the nerpa, which will dive up to 985 feet (300 m) in search of this fatty treat.

DID YOU KNOW?

Nerpas spend most of the winter under Lake Baikal's *frozen surface.* They build vast networks of air holes and *poke their noses out periodically to breathe.*

Living up to **56 years**, the nerpa has the *longest lifespan of any seal* in the world.

Smooth-Coated Otter

Found in the rivers of India, China, and Indonesia, smooth-coated otters also depend on fish for survival. These 4-foot (1.2-m) mammals live in family groups of up to 17 members. The families hunt together, surrounding schools of fish and driving them into small areas. When enough fish have been corralled, individual otters take turns grabbing mouthfuls of the fish "soup."

Otters are hunted by larger predators. To keep themselves safe, otters screech and hiss when they see a predator approaching. The other family members soon rush over, and the group harasses the predator until it gives up and moves away.

DID YOU KNOW?

Smooth-coated otters are considered the **world's most social otter species.**

Otters are territorial. They use musk glands at the bases of their tails to *mark favorite feeding and resting spots.*

PLANET QUIZ

An adult otter weighs about 24 pounds (11 kg). In one day, what percentage of this weight does the otter eat in food?

a) 1/8   b) 1/4

c) 1/2   d) 3/4

Answer: a) One-eighth. An adult otter eats approximately 3 pounds (1.4 kg) of fish, frogs, rats, turtles, birds, and other animals each day.

59

Sockeye Salmon

Measuring about 33 inches (84 cm) in length and weighing up to 15 pounds (7 kg), these big fish spend a few years taking it easy in the open ocean. But then it comes time for the salmon to leave the ocean and swim upriver, searching for the exact spot where they hatched years earlier.

After a long journey, the sockeye salmon reach their destinations. Females lay eggs and males fertilize them. Then the adult salmon die, leaving crayfish, eagles, bears, and hosts of other animals to enjoy the seafood feast.

DID YOU KNOW?

Sockeye salmon flesh is **bright orange**. It gets this color from krill, which the salmon eats in huge numbers *during its ocean-living years.*

There are *five species of Pacific salmon* in addition to the sockeye. **Depending on the species,** these fish *can be found anywhere* from the northwest Pacific to Korea, China, and Japan.

Thousands of years ago, a single cichlid species somehow got stranded in Africa's Lake Malawi. *All of today's 850 species evolved from this ancestor.*

Cichlid parents educate their babies. They show them how to *nibble algae off leaves, dig in the soil with their fins for food,* and many other survival tactics.

Cichlid

Like the sockeye salmon, small fish called cichlids are known for their unusual breeding techniques. Males build underwater structures, such as pits or mounds, in Africa's great freshwater lakes. If the females like what they see, they lay eggs. The male fertilizes the eggs, then sucks them gently into his large mouth. He will carry the eggs until they hatch.

The male's job is not done when the young fish, called fry, emerge. At the first sign of a predator, he signals the fry to swim back into his mouth. The father will protect his babies in this way until they are large enough to protect themselves.

PLANET QUIZ

True or false? Because they are so isolated, cichlid populations are more stable than those of most fish.

Answer: False. There have been close to 50 cichlid extinctions in recent years. An additional 182 species are thought to be in trouble. Cichlids and other animals that live in small, specific locations are very sensitive to environmental threats.

seasonal forests

Certain regions are warm in the summer and cool in the winter. These areas offer perfect growing conditions for trees, the Earth's mightiest plants. From the majestic moose to the world's smallest cat, animals of every size and type roam the vast seasonal forests of Planet Earth.

Moose

Many large animals live in our planet's northern forests. The biggest of them all is the moose, which measures up to 6.5 feet (2 m) at the shoulder and weighs an incredible 1,600 pounds (726 kg).

It's impossible to miss this animal's antlers, which the moose uses as a weapon against predators. Recent research suggests that the antlers may also act like hearing aids, bouncing sound waves into the moose's ears. This is useful on the tundra, where there are very few trees. Extra-sensitive hearing gives the moose a big advantage in this wide-open environment.

DID YOU KNOW?

The moose is the official animal *of the state of Maine.*

The moose's antlers are called **the rack**. *The spikes on the antlers are called tines.*

Pudu

You could lay two pudu end-to-end across the moose's mighty antlers. Just 14 inches (35 cm) tall at the shoulder, these little animals are native to South America, where they roam dense forests and the nearby grasslands.

With their small size, pudus make easy targets for predators. To stay safe, these animals have developed plenty of quick-escape skills. They are excellent runners, jumpers, and swimmers. A pudu can even scramble up leaning tree trunks to get away from danger.

PLANET QUIZ

The word "velvet" refers to the soft skin that covers a pudu's

    a) Nose   b) Antlers

    c) Rump   d) Hooves

Answer: b) Antlers. All deer produce this unique skin. The velvet covers and protects the antlers while they are growing. When the antlers are fully developed, the velvet peels off.

Lynx

Measuring about 40 inches (1 m) in length and weighing up to 44 pounds (20 kg), the lynx is a lot of cat. Found in the forests of North America, Eurasia, and Spain, these creatures can be recognized by their black ear tufts and stubby, black-tipped tails. The chances of ever catching a glimpse of these features are extremely slim. Lynx are particularly shy, and they stay out of the way when humans approach.

The snowshoe hare isn't so lucky. These animals make up the biggest part of the Canada lynx's diet. The lynx depends so much on hares, in fact, that its population falls in years when this prey is scarce.

DID YOU KNOW?

Lynx have very large feet. The toes spread out when they hit the ground, *allowing the feet to act like natural snowshoes.*

The Iberian lynx is found only in Spain. With an estimated population of 120 individuals, **it is the most endangered of all lynx species.**

DID YOU KNOW?

Kodkods avoid bright, open places at all costs. One kodkod was seen waiting several hours to cross a sunlit path. *The cat did not emerge until a shadow fell across the area.*

Kodkod

Like the lynx, the kodkod cat of Chile and Argentina prefers to stay hidden. Thanks to its tiny body, it has no problem reaching this goal. Just 16 inches (40 cm) long and weighing as little as 4.5 pounds (2 kg), these felines roam at night, slipping silently through dense bushes as they search for prey.

These cats prefer to hunt small animals, filling their bellies with birds, lizards, and even insects. Sightings suggest that kodkods are also tempted by pudu, but they are an ambitious target. The world's smallest deer outweighs the kodkod by a huge margin.

Wolverine

Measuring up to 34 inches (86 cm) in length and weighing up to 44 pounds (20 kg), wolverines live in far northern forest environments, where they terrorize animals of all sizes with their aggressive hunting techniques.

Besides being fierce hunters, wolverines are also huge eaters. In relation to its size, this creature can gulp down more food in one sitting than

DID YOU KNOW?

Wolverines usually prey on small animals. However, they can and will take down prey five times their own size *if the opportunity arises.*

During the wintertime, *the flesh of dead*

Periodical Cicada

For a true display of gluttony, you'll need to enter a temperate forest during the swarming phase of the periodical cicada. These 1.5-inch (4-cm) insects develop underground for periods of 13 or 17 years. At the end of this period, the cicadas emerge in a frenzy of breeding. After three to four weeks they will die, leaving the forest littered with their carcasses.

Cicadas eat little to nothing during their short lives. But they're probably the only creatures in the area *not* chowing down. During one cicada emergence, scientists saw birds too full to fly and chipmunks gorged to the point of throwing up!

DID YOU KNOW?

For the cicada, **group emergence is a survival strategy.** Millions of cicadas may get eaten, *but millions more survive to ensure the survival of the species.*

In the years that cicadas emerge, the local trees enjoy a growth spurt. *This happens partly because the sap-sucking cicada nymphs have left the soil,* and partly because cicada carcasses return vital nutrients *to the forest floor.*

PLANET QUIZ

The process by which an immature insect suddenly reaches adult form is called:

a) Transformation   b) Pupation

c) Metamorphosis   d) Corpogenesis

Answer: c) Metamorphosis. Many insects go through this process, which usually results in a change of habitat, behavior, and looks.

caves

Beneath our feet lies a hidden world. Filled with water and air, these shafts, passages, and caverns make up the habitat known as caves. Plants cannot survive here. But animals can and many do.

Wrinkle-Lipped Bat

Just before twilight, tourists gather outside Deer Cave in Borneo for the nightly exit of the cave's wrinkle-lipped bats. Between 5:30 and 6:30 p.m., millions of these winged mammals swarm out of the cave, hunting for the insects that make up their diet.

Wings included, wrinkle-lipped bats are not much wider than an outstretched human hand. By open-air standards, they are tiny. In the cave world, however, these animals are giants. They dwarf the cockroaches, spiders, and other small creatures that lurk in the underground darkness.

DID YOU KNOW?

Along with their eyesight, Belizean white crabs have also lost their pigmentation. *Animals that spend their lives in the darkness have no need for bold shades or patterns.*

Even in caves, **Belizean white crabs are hunted by other animals.** They spend most of their time *hiding behind rocks to avoid this threat.*

Belizean White Crab

While bats head for the open air each night, Belizean white crabs stay put. They have to. Found in just one cave system in Belize, these small crustaceans have lived in the darkness so long that they have lost the ability to see.

Since they are stuck in one place, white crabs can't go looking for food. Fortunately, well-fed bats pass waste called guano. The crabs eat this waste, which contains plenty of leftover

PLANET QUIZ

The Belizean white crab is an omnivore. This means it eats:

a) Waste matter   b) Plant matter

c) Animal matter   d) Anything it can find

caves

DID YOU KNOW?

Like bats, cave swiftlets use echolocation. They are one of only two birds to have this ability. *The other is the oilbird, a South American avian that also spends time in caves.*

Because they are born in the dark, young swiftlets never see their parents *during the early weeks of their lives.*

Cave Swiftlet

The legs and feet of cave swiftlets are so small that they cannot perch. It's a dangerous situation for this 6-inch (15-cm) bird, which is preyed upon by falcons, owls, crows, and even one particularly nasty cricket. But the little swiftlet has found an ingenious solution to its problem. It makes its home in caves, where it is a giant instead of a

Cave Glowworm

Like the cave swiftlet, the 1-inch (2.5-cm) glowworm also puts its spit to good use. Found on cave ceilings in New Zealand and Australia, these animals create long, mucus-covered threads to snare passing insects. A glowworm sits patiently, dangling its thread, until it feels a tug. The glowworm then reels in its line and eats its unlucky prey alive.

Glowworms have another weapon in their bag of tricks. They can combine two chemicals inside their abdomens to create a blue-green glow. Flying insects are attracted to the glowworms' lights, and when they fly closer, they become trapped in the glowworms' sticky "webs."

DID YOU KNOW?

The glowworm's light gives off almost no heat. It is thought to be *nearly 100 percent energy efficient.*

Despite their name, **glowworms are not worms.** They are gnat larvae. *They often catch and eat their own adult relatives,* who mature in the same caves where glowworm larvae hunt.

PLANET QUIZ

The production of light by living organisms is called:

a) Chemiluminescence

b) Bioluminescence

c) Organoluminescence

d) Physiluminescence

Answer: b) Bioluminescence. Bioluminescence is extremely common in the oceans, where an estimated 80 to 90 percent of the animals can produce light. It is less common on land, but it can be seen in fireflies and a few other insects as well as glowworms.

DID YOU KNOW?

People who are bitten by cave centipedes may **experience pain**, swelling, chills, fever, or weakness.

Female cave centipedes **guard their eggs against predators**. When the eggs hatch, the *females protect the little centipedes until they are big enough to survive on their own.*

Cave Centipede

Common garden centipedes are about as long as a human finger. Underground, however, a lack of predators has allowed cave centipedes to grow up to 12 inches (30.5 cm) in length.

Most cave centipedes feed on insects, but one South American species has found a way to take larger prey. This predator crawls to the center of the cave's ceiling. It stays there, clinging tightly with its strong legs, until an unlucky bat comes too close. Then, lightning-quick, the centipede stabs the bat with its deadly pinchers.

Cave Molly

Some cave dwellers, like the centipede, produce poison. Others swim in it. This is the case with the cave molly, a 1-inch (2.5-cm) fish found only in Mexico's Villa Luz cave. The walls and ceilings of this cave drip with powerful acid. Yet according to researchers, the little fish are so numerous that they can be scooped up by the handfuls.

There is a reason cave mollies are so abundant. Villa Luz teems with sulfur-eating bacteria and the mollies are perfectly adapted to feast on it. With a never-ending food supply, it's no wonder these small fish are thriving.

PLANET QUIZ

True or false? Centipedes travel slowly and carefully. If they walk too quickly, their many legs get tangled up.

Answer: False. Centipedes move very quickly. They are among the fastest and most agile of all non-flying bugs.

conclusion

As you have seen in this book, our home planet is a place of extremes. Some of Earth's habitats, such as the rainforests and the shallow seas, are gentle. Others, such as the deserts and the poles, are incredibly harsh. But every climate provides opportunities for adaption and survival. Over billions of years, creatures big and small have emerged to fill our planet's many ecological niches.

For tips on how to be more Earth-friendly, look at the last page of the book!

But alarmingly, within the next few years the world itself may never look the same again. Threats against these amazing creatures and their habitats can be changed — and you can help by learning about the world around you. You have taken the first step!

our world, our home

From frozen poles to humid rainforests, our extraordinary world is full of astonishing discoveries. The best part is that there's still more to learn about the world around us! But unfortunately, many of these natural wonders are in danger. Habitats are threatened, and many animals hover near extinction. We all live on Planet Earth, and it is important to keep learning about the world around us, and to support conservation efforts. But there are some things that you can do in your everyday life, too!

- **Bring Your Own Bag.** If you're going shopping, bring your own reusable bags with you. Plastic bags are made from petroleum (aka oil) and paper bags are made from trees. So if you bring your own bag, you won't be wasting either!

- **Don't Leave the Fridge Open.** Try to decide what you want before you open the fridge or freezer door — that way all the cold air won't escape.

- **Down the Tubes.** Turn off the faucet when you're brushing your teeth! You'll save lots of water from going down the drain.

- **Line Dry Your Laundry.** Hang your laundry on an old-fashioned clothesline instead of using an energy-guzzling dryer. You will save lots of energy and you'll lower your parents' electric bill, too!

- **Unplug It.** Unplug all your chargers when you're not using them. Chargers suck up energy even when you're not charging anything, so by pulling the plug, you'll be saving energy.

- **Buy Recycled.** Encourage your parents to buy recycled paper products for your house.

- **Just Say No to Plastic Water Bottles.** Instead of using disposable plastic water bottles, get a reusable container to bring water with you. Tossing out plastic water bottles creates a huge amount of waste.

- **Reusable Containers Rule.** When it comes to your lunch, the less packaging, the better. Individually wrapped snacks and drinks waste resources. Instead, use reusable containers from home to bring your food to and from school.

- **Ban Styrofoam Products.** Styrofoam never decomposes, making it an environmentally unfriendly choice. Instead of using disposable Styrofoam products, use reusable ones. The Earth will thank you.

- **Put Your Computer to Sleep.** Using a screensaver on your computer uses more energy than if you let it go to sleep. So change the preferences on your computer and give it a rest.

- **Watch out for E-Waste.** E-waste, or discarded cell phones and computers, is a growing problem. Keep electronics for as long as possible, and dispose of them responsibly. You can find an organization that will donate your old electronics to be refurbished.

- **Remember the Three R's.** Reduce. Reuse. Recycle. These are important ways to cut down on consumption and waste.

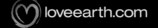 loveearth.com